F★CUS ON
Writing Composition
3

Ray Barker   Louis Fidge

Stories by significant children's authors	Trad. tales, myths, other cultures	Stories from other cultures	Plays	Concrete poetry	Classic poetry	Narrative poetry	Poems from other cultures	Choral performance poetry	Recounts	Observational records and reports	Instructional texts	Explanations	Persuasive writing
FICTION									NON-FICTION				
✔									✔	✔		✔	
✔													
✔									✔				
					✔	✔							
					✔			✔					
			✔										
									✔			✔	
									✔		✔	✔	
									✔	✔		✔	
												✔	✔
	✔	✔											
	✔	✔											
				✔	✔			✔					
✔										✔			
									✔	✔		✔	
✔												✔	
✔									✔				
✔							✔	✔					
									✔	✔		✔	✔
									✔			✔	
												✔	✔
											✔	✔	✔

Contents

UNIT 1   A Reading Log

Think ahead

Why do you think it is useful to record what you have read? People call these records 'logs' or 'journals'. How much information do you think it is necessary to give in your reading log? What sort of things should you record? Who is going to read the log?

My Reading Log on the Environment
by Amit Mukherji

My interest is in finding out about our environment. I think this is important because we only have one world. Many animals are nearly extinct. Pollution is a real problem. I think we need to learn about the problems so we can do something about them. I found these books in the library which told me more about the environment.

Fiction	Non-fiction
The Water Horse Dick King-Smith published by Viking	**Ecology** Richard Spurgeon published by Usborne
Pig in the Middle Sam Llewellyn published by Walker	**Why Are People Hungry?** Ruth Versfeld published by Watts
Little Foxes Michael Morpurgo published by Mammoth	**Wind Energy** Graham Rickard published by Wayland
Mrs Frisby and the Rats of NIMH Robert C O'Brien published by Gollancz	**What A Load of Rubbish!** Steve Skidmore published by Cassell
Why the Whales Came Michael Morpurgo published by Heinemann	**Global Warming** Laurence Pringle published by Hodder and Stoughton

Reading Log for Amit Mukherji

Date: Spring Term
Subject: The Environment
Book: Why the Whales Came
Author: Michael Morpurgo
Type of book: Fiction

What is the book about?

I loved this book. The story is set in 1914. There is a mystery about the Island of Samson. The children meet a deaf man called the Birdman on the next island. The children are trapped on Samson Island one day and find a strange horn. When the war starts the people think the Birdman is a spy just because he is different. The Birdman tries to rescue a trapped whale. The story shows how important the whales are to our world.

What are the characters like?

Gracie and Daniel are not prejudiced. They go to talk to the old man who is deaf. He carves birds. They know he is not a spy. They try to rescue the whales and stop Daniel's brother from killing them.

What I thought of this book.

The book is interesting. The characters are very realistic. The whales do not come until the end. In 1914, they did not know about the environment. The story shows us how we need to live with the whales and not kill them.

Reading Log for Amit Mukherji

Date: Summer Term
Subject: The Environment
Book: What a Load of Rubbish!
Author: Steve Skidmore
Type of book: Non-fiction

What is the book about?

This book is about the rubbish in the world and what we can do with it. The author tells us what problems it causes in the world. He shows us how recycling can help the world.

Is it easy to understand the information?

It is simple to understand. The author does not use difficult words. He writes as if he is talking to you. There are lots of cartoons and silly facts.

What I thought of this book.

I like this book because it is funny. I think the way he gives us loads of information is great. It makes me feel that I am responsible for causing some of the world's problems. But it also shows me that I can do something about it. For example, I can separate out my rubbish for recycling. Perhaps they could have put less on the page so it looked better.

Thinking back

1 Look at Amit's first list.
   a) What else did he write down besides the title of the book?
   b) Why might this information be useful?
2 In reading logs: a) Why is a date important?
   b) Why do you think Amit did not write more about these books?
   c) Give two reasons why Amit liked the fiction book.
   d) What does Amit think could be better about the non-fiction title?

 Thinking about it

Design a poster to tell others in your class about one of Amit's books. Your job is to tell others in a brief way what Amit thought of the book. Include:
– the title, the author and the type of book;
– a brief account of what it is about;
– its good points and any not so good points;
– what Amit really thinks of it.
Do a rough copy first in pencil so you can experiment with your ideas.
Remember, keep it simple. Use pictures as well.

 Thinking it through

Choose a subject in which you are interested. It could be one you are working through in class, such as Space or Ancient Egypt.
– Make a reading list, like Amit's, of books you have found about your subject. You may have to visit the library.
– Read two of these books – a fiction title and a non-fiction title – and write a reading log about each one. Copymaster 1 will help you plan this.

Stepping Stones to help you

• Write the title and the author of the book.
• Explain why you read the book.
• Write a brief summary of the plot or subject matter.
• Write about characters or say how information is presented.
• Give your opinion of the book.
(Use copymaster A to help you.)

UNIT 2 New Scenes in the Style of a Writer

Think ahead

Books are different from each other because they are each written in a different way, or style. What makes this passage so different from anything else you have read? Do you think it is funny or confusing? Why?

Milo and his dog, Tock, are lost in Dictionopolis, where words come from. They meet the king's advisers.

"We are the king's advisers, or, in more formal terms, his cabinet."

"Cabinet," recited the duke: "(1) a small private room or closet, case with drawers, etc., for keeping valuables or displaying curiosities; (2) council room for chief ministers of state; (3) a body of official advisers to the chief executive of a nation."

"You see," continued the minister, bowing thankfully to the duke, "Dictionopolis is the place where all the words in the world come from. They're grown right here in our orchards."

"I didn't know that words grew on trees," said Milo timidly.

"Where did you think they grew?" shouted the earl irritably.

A small crowd began to gather to see the little boy who didn't know that letters grew on trees.

"I didn't know they grew at all," admitted Milo even more timidly. Several people shook their heads sadly.

"Well, money doesn't grow on trees, does it?" demanded the count.

"I've heard not," said Milo.

"Then something must. Why not words?" exclaimed the under-secretary triumphantly. The crowd cheered his display of logic and continued about its business.

"To continue," continued the minister impatiently. "Once a week by Royal Proclamation the word market is held here in the great square, and people

7

come from everywhere to buy the words they need or trade in the words they haven't used."

"Our job," said the count, "is to see that all the words sold are proper ones, for it wouldn't do to sell someone a word that had no meaning or didn't exist at all. For instance, if you bought a word like *ghlbtsk*, where would you use it?"

"It would be difficult," thought Milo – but there were so many words that were difficult, and he knew hardly any of them.

"But we never choose which ones to use," explained the earl as they walked towards the market stalls, "for as long as they mean what they mean to mean we don't care if they make sense or nonsense."

"Innocence or magnificence," added the count.

"Reticence or common sense," said the under-secretary.

"That seems simple enough," said Milo, trying to be polite.

"Easy as falling off a log," cried the earl, falling off a log with a loud thump.

"Must you be so clumsy?" shouted the duke.

"All I said was –" began the earl, rubbing his head.

"We heard you," said the minister angrily, "and you'll have to find an expression that's less dangerous."

The earl dusted himself, as the others snickered audibly.

"You see," cautioned the count, "you must pick your words very carefully and be sure to say what you intend to say. And now we must leave to make preparations for the Royal Banquet."

From *The Phantom Tollbooth* by Norton Juster

 Thinking back

1 a) What strange thing happens when the advisers mention the word 'cabinet'?
   b) Which of the three meanings is correct to describe the advisers?
   c) Find another example of this happening in the passage.
2 Explain where words come from in Dictionopolis.
3 Why do people come to the word market every week?
4 What is the job of the king's advisers?

Thinking about it

Continue the story where Milo and Tock meet people from Dictionopolis in the market. Remember the people in the market should talk about words in the same way. For example, they should define all the words like a dictionary when they use them. Use copymaster 2 to help you collect words. You will need a dictionary and a thesaurus.

- Describe what the market will look like, sound like, smell like.
- Describe the people you meet. Do they look the same as us?
- Which words have they come to collect at the market and why?
- Write down their speech to make the story livelier.
- What will make the story amusing?

Use the Stepping Stones to help you draft your work.

 Thinking it through

Use the same style of writing to tell the story of what happens later at the Royal Banquet. Make the story amusing. Use copymaster 2, a dictionary and a thesaurus to help you plan which words to use.

- What is the king like?
- What is the palace like?
- How do the characters talk?
- What happens if Milo mentions a nonsense word, such as *ghlbtsk*?
- Use proverbs to make the events funny, for example when someone says: "Easy as falling off a log," someone falls off a log! What would happen if Milo said: "It rained cats and dogs"?
- Use lots of speech, as in the passage.

Stepping Stones to help you

- Decide on the audience for your writing.
- The language of your writing should be right for your audience.
- Think carefully about the purpose of your writing.
- Decide on the form of the writing. Will it be a diary? a letter? a story?
- Check your grammar and punctuation before you produce your final copy.

(Use copymasters B and R to help you.)

UNIT 3 New Characters in the Style of a Writer

Think ahead

We like many stories because of the characters in them. What kinds of characters are in this extract – are they pleasant or unpleasant? Which characters do you admire? Are the characters really believable or just comic?

Miss Jennifer Honey was a mild and quiet person who never raised her voice and was seldom seen to smile, but there is no doubt she possessed that rare gift for being adored by every small child under her care. She seemed to understand totally the bewilderment and fear that so often overwhelms young children who for the first time in their lives are herded into a classroom and told to obey orders. Some curious warmth that was almost tangible shone out of Miss Honey's face when she spoke to a confused and homesick newcomer to the class.

Miss Trunchbull, the Headmistress, was something else altogether. She was a gigantic holy terror, a fierce tyrannical monster who frightened the life out of the pupils and teachers alike. There was an aura of menace about her even at a distance, and when she came up close you could almost feel the dangerous heat radiating from her as from a red-hot rod of metal. When she marched – Miss Trunchbull never walked, she always marched like a storm trooper with long strides and arms aswinging – when she marched along a corridor you could actually hear her snorting as she went, and if a group of children happened to be in her path, she ploughed right on through them like a tank, with small people bouncing off her to left and right. Thank goodness we don't meet many people like her in this world, although they do exist and all of us are likely to come across at least one of them in a lifetime. If you ever do, you should behave as you would if you met an enraged rhinoceros out in the bush – climb up the nearest tree and stay there until it has gone away. This woman, in all her eccentricities and in her appearance, is almost impossible to describe, but I shall make some attempt to do so a little later on. Let us leave her for the moment and go back to Matilda and her first day in Miss Honey's class.

After the usual business of going through all the names of the children, Miss Honey handed out a brand-new exercise-book to each pupil.

'You have all brought your own pencils, I hope,' she said.

'Yes, Miss Honey,' they chanted.

'Good. Now this is the very first day of school for each one of you. It is the beginning of at least eleven long years of schooling that all of you are going to have to go through. And six of those years will be spent right here at Crunchem Hall where, as you know, your Headmistress is Miss Trunchbull. Let me for your own good tell you something about Miss Trunchbull. She insists upon strict discipline throughout the school, and if you take my advice you will do your very best to behave yourselves in her presence. Never argue with her. Never answer her back. Always do as she says. If you get on the wrong side of Miss Trunchbull she can liquidise you like a carrot in a kitchen blender. It's nothing to laugh about, Lavender. Take that grin off your face. All of you will be wise to remember that Miss Trunchbull deals very very severely with anyone who gets out of line in this school. Have you got the message?'

'Yes, Miss Honey,' chirruped eighteen eager little voices.

'I myself', Miss Honey went one, 'want to help you to learn as much as possible while you are in this class. That is because I know it will make things easier for you later on.'

From *Matilda* by Roald Dahl

Thinking back

1 How do you know the author admired Miss Honey?
2 Explain why the author thinks Miss Honey is such a good teacher.
3 What things does the author compare Miss Trunchbull to in order to show her nastiness?
4 How can you tell Miss Trunchbull is cruel by the way she behaves?

 Thinking about it

1 Make notes about the characters of Miss Honey and Miss Trunchbull from the passage. Copymaster 3 will help you record what you find in the passage. For instance,

Miss Honey:	mild and quiet – never raises her voice
Miss Trunchbull:	fierce and cruel – frightens children

2 Now write about what sort of personality each of them has. Is what ways are they different? The Stepping Stones will help.

 Thinking it through

Miss Honey tells Matilda that Miss Trunchbull is very strict and never to 'get on her wrong side'. Write an episode from the story in which the clever Matilda gets her revenge on Miss Trunchbull. Make this very funny. Introduce new characters to help in Matilda's plan.
– Use copymaster 3 to plan the characters.
– What does Matilda do to get the better of Miss Trunchbull?
– How does she carry out her plan and how does it succeed?
– What happens to Matilda?

(Stepping Stones to help you)

Think about these things:
    What does the character look like?
    How does the character behave?
    What does the character say?
Use good describing words to make your character interesting.
(Use copymaster C to help you.)

UNIT 4   Poems about Moods and Feelings

Think ahead

This poem describes what it is like when it snows. How does snow change the way we see things? hear things? feel things? How does the way the poet describes these things help you to imagine them?

London Snow

When men were all asleep the snow came flying,
In large white flakes falling on the city brown,
Stealthily and perpetually★ settling and loosely lying,   ★going on forever
Hushing the latest traffic of the drowsy town;
Deadening, muffling, stifling its murmurs failing;
Lazily and incessantly★ floating down and down: ★without stopping
Silently sifting and veiling road, roof and railing;
Hiding difference, making unevenness even,
Into angles and crevices softly drifting and sailing.

All night it fell, and when full inches seven
It lay in the depth of its uncompacted lightness,
The clouds blew off from a high and frosty heaven;
And all woke earlier for the unaccustomed brightness
Of the winter dawning, the strange unheavenly glare:
The eye marvelled – marvelled at the dazzling whiteness;
The ear harkened★ to the stillness of the solemn air;   ★listened
No sound of wheel rumbling nor of foot falling,
And the busy morning cries came thin and spare.

Then boys I heard, as they went to school, calling,
They gathered up the crystal manna★ to freeze   ★a kind of food
Their tongues with tasting, their hands with snowballing;
Or rioted in a drift, plunging up to the knees;
Or peering up from under the white-mossed wonder,
"O look at the trees!" they cried, "O look at the trees!"

From *London Snow* by Robert Bridges

Thinking back

1 Explain what London was like when it snowed that night.
2 Find three words which prove that the snow made everything quieter.
3 a) How did the boys feel when they woke up? Why?
   b) Explain how these lines change the mood of the poem.
4 a) What did the boys do with the snow on their way to school?
   b) Would you do the same things?

Thinking about it

1 Copy out the first verse of the poem. Underline all the words which contain an 's' sound. Repeating this sound helps to create mood and feelings of soft snow. Is the sound a hard or a soft sound?
2 Now, circle all the 'ing' endings. How many are there? Repeating this ending gives us the idea of the snow coming down, without stopping.
3 Use copymaster 4 to sort out words which have hard and soft sounds.
4 Write four more lines describing snow using soft-sounding words only.
– Describe what it looks like, what it feels like, what it sounds like.
– Your lines do not have to rhyme.
  Use the Stepping Stones to help you.

Thinking it through

Write a poem about everything freezing one icy night. Use hard-sounding words only to create the mood – perhaps using 'k', 'g' or 'c' sounds.
Your poem does not have to rhyme. Collect together words which create the right mood and feelings. Think about some of these ideas.
– Icicles: hard, sharp, pointy like daggers or stalactites.
– Ice on water: cracks when you step on it; hard surface to walk on.
– The world seems to have stopped – frozen in time.
– The ice dies when the sun rises.

Stepping Stones to help you

- Decide what type of poem you want to write.
- Make rough notes of your ideas and choose only the best ones.
- Use your notes to make a first draft.
- Check on the ideas, spelling and punctuation and make a final draft.
(Use copymaster Q to help you.)

UNIT 5   Using Metaphor: Personification

Think ahead

A 'metaphor' is a comparison. It says something is something else, for example: the road was a snake winding through the desert. *'Personification' is a kind of metaphor. This is when something is compared to a person, as in this poem. What is thunder compared to? How does the poem explain why there is thunder?*

Giant Thunder

Giant Thunder, striding home,
Wonders if his supper's done.

"Hag wife, hag wife, bring me my bones!"
"They are not done," the old hag moans.

"Not done? Not done?" the giant roars
And heaves his old wife out of doors.

Cries he, "I'll have them, cooked or not!"
But overturns the cooking pot.

He flings the burning coals about;
See how the lightning flashes out!

Upon the gale the old hag rides,
The cloudy moon for terror hides.

All the world with thunder quakes;
Forest shudders, mountain shakes;
From the cloud the rainstorm breaks;
Village ponds are turned to lakes;
Every living creature wakes.

Hungry Giant, lie you still!
Stamp no more, from hill to hill –
Tomorrow you shall have your fill.

From *Giant Thunder* by James Reeves

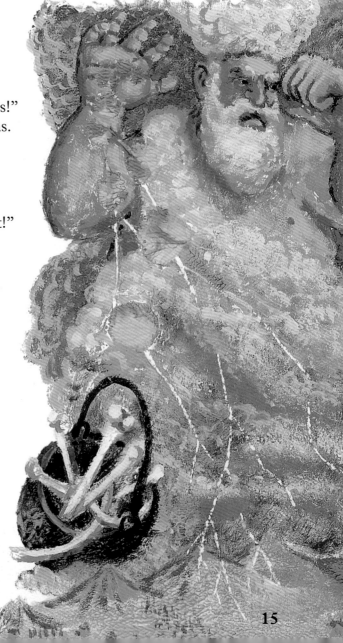

Thinking back

1 What is Thunder described as in the first line?
2 Why does the poet say Thunder gets angry?
3 What does the poet say causes: a) the lightning? b) the thunder?
4 Give three examples of the effect that thunder has on the world.
5 How does the poet explain that the thunder will stop by tomorrow?

 Thinking about it

1 Copy and complete the chart about Thunder in the poem.

Word in the poem	Meaning	Human features
strides	walks	has legs
wonders	thinks	has a brain
moans		

2 Think of some more metaphors that could make Thunder and his wife human. Here are some ideas.
    – Fingers: lightning pointing at the ground.
    – Hands: tear down trees in a storm.
    – Hair: white clouds in the sky.
Write four more lines about Thunder, using personification.

 Thinking it through

Write a poem about fog. Use copymaster 5 to help you.
– The poem must compare the fog to a person.
– It should describe its actions and movement as if it were a person.
– It should mention parts of the human body.
– Describe: what you can see – is there any colour? what you can hear – are sounds altered? what you can taste or smell.

(Stepping Stones to help you)

• A metaphor is a comparison, but it does not use 'like' or 'as'.
• Personification – this happens when you give human qualities and feelings to ideas or objects.
• A 'simile' is a comparison, but it uses 'like' or 'as'.
(Use copymaster D to help you.)

UNIT 6 Writing a Playscript

Think ahead

A 'playscript' is a way of writing down dialogue for a performance on a stage. Is it meant to be read or performed? How are the words written differently from a story?

ACT 1
Scene I
The time of the Ancient Romans. A jungle scene. The roar of lions. Along the path comes a lion. He is limping. He roars in pain. He lifts one paw. A large thorn sticks out of it. He licks it. He shakes it. It will not come out. He roars again. Tears fall from his eyes. He limps off the path and falls asleep under a bush.

Androcles and his wife come along. He is little and thin. She is large and tall. He is carrying all the luggage. She has a stick to help her. They are both tired.

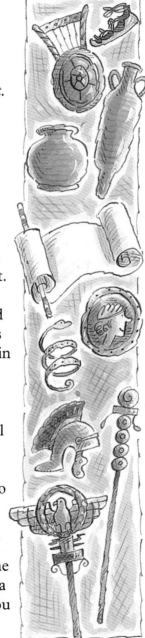

WIFE: I won't walk another step. *(She throws her stick on the ground.)*

ANDROCLES: Please dear. *(He drops the luggage.)* It's no use having a tantrum. We need to get to the village before night. They say there are wild beasts in this wood.

WIFE: I don't believe what you say. You wouldn't know a wild beast if there was one right next to you now. You are always threatening me with wild beasts. I can hardly put one foot in front of the other. I'm so tired. You cruel brute. *(She kicks the luggage.)* You don't love me. All you think of is yourself. Self! Self! Self! *(She kicks him and sits on the luggage.)*

ANDROCLES: *(He sits on the ground. He strokes his leg.)* We all think of ourselves sometimes, dear. After all, you make me think of you a great deal!

WIFE: What? *(She turns to him.)* Is it my fault I am married to you?

ANDROCLES: No dear. *(Quietly under his breath.)* That's my fault.

WIFE: You make us a laughing stock. You won't sacrifice to the gods. You have to be a Christian. How is a woman to keep a house when you bring in every lost animal you can find? You took the bread out of my mouth to feed them.

ANDROCLES: But ….

WIFE: *(She shouts.)* Don't deny it!

ANDROCLES: Only when they were hungry and you were getting too fat, dear.

WIFE: You insult me! *(She stands up. She towers above him.)* I won't bear it another moment. You talk to dumb beasts for hours. You never talk to me. You'll be sorry when I'm eaten by wild beasts. *(She dashes off into the jungle and trips over the sleeping lion.)* Oh! Andy, Andy, Andy! *(She faints. She lands on Androcles behind her. She pins him to the ground.)*

ANDROCLES: *(Creeping out from under her.)* What is it my precious? *(She wakes and points into the bushes.)* I'll go and see. *(The lion roars. Androcles faints. He falls on top of his wife and wakes.)* Did you sssss…see…aaaa…lllll…lion?

WIFE: It's all your fault. *(She hits him again.)* It's a punishment from the gods because you are a Christian. *(The lion roars again. Wife faints.)*

ANDROCLES: I'll go to him. It will take him ages to eat me. I'm stringy and tough. He won't want my wife then. *(The lion roars. Androcles shakes. The lion holds up his injured paw.)* Oh! You're lame. Poor thing. He's got a thorn in his paw. Did um get a thorny in um's tootsums wootsums? *(Androcles moves to the lion and picks up his paw. The lion roars.)* Yes, that's right. Be out in a minute. Hold it steady. That's it! *(The lion roars and shakes his paw. He licks Androcles' face.)* Yes, kissums Andy Wandy. Stop it! It tickles!

WIFE: *(Waking up.)* Oh, you coward. You haven't kissed me for years!

Adapted from *Androcles and the Lion* by George Bernard Shaw

Thinking back

1 Find ways in which this playscript is different from speech in a story.

Playscript	Story
Does not use speech marks.	

2 What sort of costumes do you think these characters would wear?
3 Find evidence to show that this play is meant to be funny.
4 How does the writer show you that the instructions for the play are not spoken by the actors?

 Thinking about it

Write the next episode of 'Androcles and the Lion' as a playscript. Use the passage and the Stepping Stones to help you use the correct style.
– Where will they go next? You will have to set the scene.
– How will his wife react? You will have to carry on with what you have learned of her character.
– How will other people react to the lion? Will they be captured? Will they escape?
– How will the lion help Androcles in return?

 Thinking it through

Write a playscript using a well-known story. Copymaster 6 will help you.
– A ballad or a narrative poem is a good source of a playscript because it normally includes exciting events and some dialogue.
– What other information will you add to make it dramatic?
– What else will you need for your performance: costumes? props?

Stepping Stones to help you

• Write the characters' names on the left. Start a new line each time a new character speaks.
• Do not use speech marks. Do not use 'he said', 'she said,' and so on.
• Use stage directions for the actions.
• Write the stage directions in brackets (or in italics with a word processor).
(Use copymaster E to help you.)

UNIT 7   Recounting Information

Think ahead

When you write an account, you need to give information as clearly as possible. What does this writer say to illustrate his facts? Which words does he use to connect together the paragraphs? Is this account clear?

The History of the Police Force

We are all used to having a police force. What would the world be like without one? We do not have to go back very far to find out.

The first police forces

Once, in 1663, the City of London employed watchmen to guard the streets at night. Later they were called 'Charlies'. They were the men who were too old to do any other kind of work. They carried a bell, a light and a rattle. They also carried a large stick to protect themselves against thieves and robbers.

At the time, life on the streets was not very safe. One person wrote in 1743, *'London is really dangerous. Pickpockets make no scruple to knock people down with sticks in Fleet Street and the Strand. You are forced to travel, even at noon, as if you are going into battle.'*

Next, in 1750, Henry Fielding began the first small detective force. He knew that for this to work he had to get the public to help. He published descriptions of criminals and asked the public to help with information. First they were called constables. Later they became known as the Bow Street Runners.

Things begin to change

In 1790, the Prime Minister, William Pitt, tried to get Parliament to set up a new police force, but no one would support him. There were too few constables to deal with crime and unrest on the streets.

Later, in 1815, the war with Napoleon and France ended. Thousands of soldiers came home without jobs or money. There were a number of riots on the streets. The most famous was in 1819 in St Peter's Field, Manchester. Eleven people were killed and 400 were injured. The government became very unpopular.

A modern police force is founded

By 1828, Robert Peel, the Home Secretary knew that a police force was essential. He started his own with 450 men in London. They were called 'Peelers' or 'Bobbies' after their founder.

This was the start of the modern police force.

Adapted from 'The History of the Police Force' from *The Story of the Police*

Thinking back

1 How do the title and the subheadings make this account clearer?
2 How does the author introduce his subject?
3 a) What dates are mentioned in the passage?
   b) Write down one fact about the police force for each date.
4 a) Why was London a dangerous place to walk around in?
   b) Why is it important to give evidence like this in an account?

Thinking about it

1 Write a paragraph about the modern-day police force.
   – Do they carry weapons?   wear uniform?   have a nickname?
   – What kind of work do they do?   – How do they solve crimes now?
   Use the Stepping Stones to help you.
2 Write about how the modern-day police force is different from the past.
   Copy and complete this chart to help you.

Police forces in the past	Modern-day police force
1663 – employed people who were too old for any other kind of work.	Highly trained.

Thinking it through

1 Write an account of a school trip. Use copymaster 7 to help you plan your work. You could write a timetable of the stages of the trip:

> 9.15   Coach arrives
> 10.00   Arrived at museum

Then note down how you felt. What made an impression on you?
2 Write about the trip   a) for your teacher   b) in a letter to a friend.

Stepping Stones to help you

• Start by setting the scene: *We are all used to having a police force …*
• Tell the events in the order in which they occurred ('chronological order').
• Give a conclusion at the end. This brings us back to the subject.
• Use the past tense and connectives which are to do with time.
(Use copymaster F to help.)

UNIT 8   Writing Instructions

Think ahead

Instructions and directions need to be clear or your reader will not know what to do. What does this writer use besides words to make his instructions clear? Why does he number his points?

In Ancient Egypt, farmers needed water to irrigate their crops. The River Nile was their main source of water. Often the river flooded.

Floodwater could be 'trapped' in reservoirs when the river sank. The fields would then have a water supply even when the river wasn't in flood. To lift the water into the fields the farmers used a shaduf. This was a trellis holding up a pole, with a counterweight on one end. On the other end was a bucket that could be lowered into the water. This invention meant that one man could lift thousands of gallons of water in a day. It was so easy to make and so successful that shadufs are still used today. You can try modelling one yourself.

Picture 1

Shock your friends with a shaduf

Egyptian peasants can make a shaduf out of tree branches; you can make yours look real by making one out of twigs.

1 Collect three straight twigs about 20 cm (or 8 inches) long. Tie them together, but not too tightly, about 3 cm (1 inch) from one end. Leave some spare string hanging loose at the knot.

2 Stand the twigs up and spread the other ends out so they make a frame or trellis (see picture 2). Push the ends into Plasticine to hold the frame steady.

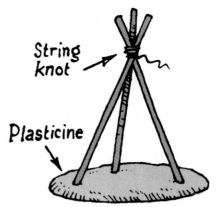

String knot

Plasticine

Picture 2

3 Find another straight twig, about 35 cm (14 inches). This will be the lever. Using the slack string, tie this to the top of the frame, where the other twigs meet. Tie the lever about 12 cm (5 inches) from one end (see picture 3).

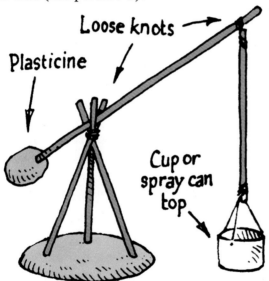

Loose knots

Plasticine

Cup or spray can top

Picture 3

4 Weight the shorter part of the lever with Plasticine.
Tie another twig, about 15 cm (6 inches) to the long end of the lever.

5 Now you need something for a bucket – the bottom of a plastic cup or the top of a spray-can would do. Make three holes in this and tie it to the twig hanging from the lever.

Congratulations – you have just made a simple but awesome invention!

'Making a shaduf' from *The Awesome Egyptians* **by Terry Deary and Peter Hepplewhite**

Thinking back

1 What are the instructions for?
2 List the things you need to make a shaduf.
3 a) Why are the instructions numbered?
 b) How does this help?
4 How do the diagrams help you understand the instructions?
5 a) List five verbs used in the instructions.
 b) What do you notice about them?

Thinking about it

Write simple instructions for a familiar everyday act, such as washing your hair or making a cup of tea.
– Copymaster 8 will help you plan this.
– Use the Stepping Stones to remind you what to do.

Thinking it through

Write directions of how to:
a) get to the front gate of the school from where you are sitting now;
b) get to school from where you live. You could also include maps.
– Follow the rules in the Stepping Stones.
– Use direction words, for example 'right', 'left' and 'straight ahead'.
– Use capitals for the names of streets and roads. Don't forget to point out landmarks, for example: *turn left by the supermarket …*
– Give your reader a sense of distance, for example: *Walk a hundred metres … Travel by bus for about two miles …*

Stepping Stones to help you

• First list what you need and explain what you are going to do.
• Follow the correct sequence of events. Number the instructions.
• Use bullet points, diagrams and labels.
• Use short sentences and verbs in the imperative (command), for example: *Take a cup … Walk along the street …*
• Write in the present tense.
(Use copymaster G.)

24

UNIT 9   Making Notes

Think ahead

Making notes helps you to remember important facts from what you have read. Notes should be short. What can you do to write down words and phrases in a shorter way? How can you write down ideas from this passage in a way which will be clear to you later?

Education in Ancient Greece

In Ancient Greece, only the sons of rich families were educated, not the daughters. In Athens, girls were kept apart from everyday life, like their mothers. They took no part in education, although some were given lessons privately at home. They were meant only to become good housewives.

Teachers were paid fees for teaching. Some were even the slaves of the household. There were no rules about when education should begin. Usually children started 'school' when they were about seven years old.

The traditional education in Greece had been for war. Homer, the poet, tells us that the hero Achilles was taught music and athletics by his tutor. Music, and also dance, were important because they gave a sense of the culture of Greece. Athletics was important because the Greeks believed that a healthy body meant a healthy mind. They thought that every citizen of Athens had to be ready to be a soldier.

In Athens, when a boy was eighteen he had two years hard training as a soldier. This was different in Sparta, where boys from the age of seven lived in military barracks and were deliberately made to lead a very hard life to see if they could survive. The historian Plutarch tells us:

"… they taught them to be contented and happy, not dainty about their food, nor fearful of the dark, nor afraid to be left alone …".

This military training was finished only when the boy had lived alone in the wild countryside for a period of time. He was expected to survive at all costs, even if this meant stealing and killing. Even the girls in Sparta were expected to be physically fit and ready to fight. They trained and competed against each other, too.

By the fifth century BC in Athens, some teachers had set up their own schools called *grammatistes*. They taught reading, writing and arithmetic. Some taught music; others taught athletics. These were the most practical things to learn to earn a living. The sons of the very wealthy families would also learn philosophy. They would learn to argue their point of view with famous thinkers of their day such as Socrates. However, this kind of talk could be dangerous. Socrates later died for his views and beliefs.

Adapted from *Greek and Roman Life* by Ian Jenkins

Thinking back

1 Write out the first sentence. Underline the most important fact.
2 a) At what age did children usually start school in Greece?
  b) How is this different from when you started school?
3 For what purpose were boys in Greece really being educated?
4 What was so different about education in Sparta?

Thinking about it

Imagine you are giving a talk to the rest of the class about education in
Ancient Greece. You need notes to remember the most important facts in
the passage. Copy and complete this chart to help you.

Paragraph	Most important facts to remember
1	Only boys had education.

– Remember, not everything in the passage is really important.
– Think about the best order in which to give the information.

Thinking it through

Think of a subject about which you are enthusiastic, such as skateboarding
or computer games. Prepare a speech to your class explaining about your
chosen subject and why it interests you. Copymaster 9 will help you.
– Collect the information you need.
– Write your speech in detail.
– Draw diagrams if it will help.
Remember, you will only have your notes to speak from.

Stepping Stones to help you

• Decide on what you are making notes about.
• Underlining the most important words and making charts are good ways
  of making notes.
• Write in your own words. Do not just copy out the passage again.
• Use abbreviations when you can.
(Use copymaster H to help you.)

UNIT 10 Using Information

Think ahead

The same information can be written in many different ways for different audiences. Who do you think is the audience for this leaflet?

GETTING STARTED ON FITNESS

Swimming for beginners

- Begin with swimming widths. Swim continuously until you feel a little puffed, then stop and rest.
- Gradually increase the number of widths without a breather: then move on to swimming lengths.
- If swimming is your only form of exercise, aim for at least 15 minutes every other day. Gradually increase the distance you cover in this time.
- Vary the stroke, because each one exercises different muscles.

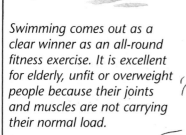

Swimming comes out as a clear winner as an all-round fitness exercise. It is excellent for elderly, unfit or overweight people because their joints and muscles are not carrying their normal load.

Cycling for beginners

- Start gradually, perhaps with five minutes on the bicycle.
- Aim for a total of about 30 minutes hard cycling about four times a week.

If cycling and jogging are combined with a few basic exercises for suppleness and strength, they are very effective. Cycling is also easy on your joints.

Jogging for beginners

- Invest in a proper pair of running shoes with cushioned soles. You can hurt your calf muscles if you don't have shoes which absorb shock.
- Make sure your gear is made of natural materials, preferably cotton – it will soak up sweat and stop chafing.
- Always warm up before you start.
- Begin with a mixture of walking and jogging – walk briskly for five minutes, then jog for 30 seconds. Carry on alternating walking and jogging for a total of ten minutes, ending up with another brisk five-minute walk.
- Gradually shorten the first walk and extend the bouts of jogging. By the end of the sixth to eighth week, you should be jogging for a good ten minutes.
- Don't be tempted to drop the second five-minute walk or "cool down" – it is important to slow down gradually.
- You should be aiming for a minimum of three 15 minute jogs a week

From The Consumers' Association

Thinking back

1 a) What is the aim of this leaflet?   b) Which audience is it written for?
2 How do the subheadings and pictures make it easier to read?
3 Why do you think the writer chose to use bullet points, and not just to write out the information in sentences?
4 Why are certain parts of the text in *italics*?

Thinking about it

Make a chart to summarise the information in this leaflet.
Make notes about:
– what you are aiming for in the exercises;
– how you start;
– what you do when you get going.
Copymaster 10 will help you make your notes.

Thinking it through

Use the information you have taken from this passage to either:
a) Write the diary of an older lady who has taken up jogging for the first time. You could begin: *Bought myself a good pair of trainers today. Running last week really hurt my calf muscles …* or
b) Write a TV script for a breakfast show advising people about the best way of taking up swimming. You could begin: *Well, Ladies and Gentlemen. I bet you thought swimming would be an easy way to get fit. Well, let us surprise you …*

Stepping Stones to help you

- Decide who you are writing the information for.
- Decide on the form of the writing. Will it be a leaflet? a poster? a set of instructions? This will affect the way in which you write it.
- Decide on the purpose of the piece of writing. Is it to make a new reference book? to persuade someone? to use with younger children?
- Plan the work carefully. Do a rough copy first.
(Use copymaster 1.)

UNIT 11   Writing Myths and Legends – Structure

Think ahead

Myths are ancient stories from all over the world. Sometimes they are like fables. They try to explain something that is a mystery. What strange things happen in this myth? What other myths does this remind you of? What kinds of characters are in this myth?

The Old Man and the Magic Bowl

The old man's life had been hard, but somehow, he had always managed to earn enough to feed himself and his wife.

With the passing years, an awful stiffness had attacked his hands and feet – and then spread with well-aimed cruelty to his legs, arms and back. He could hardly move, let alone go out to work.

He could not pay his rent, so he lost his house and had to live in a hut. He could not work for a living, so he and his wife began to starve.

When the Nine Days' Festival arrived, the old man felt more depressed than ever. He was standing listlessly by the roadside when a friend of his passed by.

"Well," said the friend, "and how are you today?"

"Not so good," replied the old man.

"Why, what is the matter?" asked his friend.

"My bones are stiff," said the old man, "I have no job and no house. My wife and I have not eaten for seven days."

"Well," said the friend, "if you take my advice …"

"Yes?" said the old man.

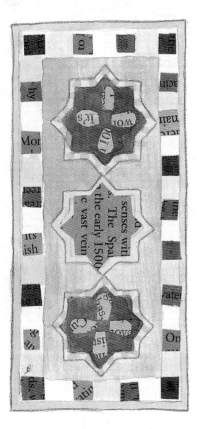

"My advice is that you go straight to Parvati's temple and throw yourself at her mercy. She is bound to help you. You had better hurry or the festival might end."

The old man could hardly hurry. With tiny, painful steps, he began the long journey towards Parvati's temple.

It was evening when he got there.

The temple was packed as were all the courtyards that surrounded it. People were spilling out into the streets.

The old man could hear the prayers and smell the far-off incense. But he could not get in.

Inside the temple, the goddess Parvati was beginning to feel uncomfortable. She turned to one of her many child-attendants and said, "Someone's problems are weighing on me like a ton of bricks. Go and find out who is in trouble and bring that person to me."

Two of the child-attendants flew around the courtyards and into the street. There they spotted the old man standing stiffly under a tree. They circled him once and made a perfect landing at his feet.

"The goddess Parvati summons you," they chanted together. Each attendant took one of the old man's hands, lifted him off the ground, and then flew him into the temple's innermost chambers. Parvati was leaning

casually against a door, her pale, beautiful face
radiating as much light as her gold sari.

"Why are you so unhappy?" she asked gently.

"Praise be to you, goddess,' the old man began as he
kneeled and touched her feet, "I have not eaten for
several days."

"Take this," said the goddess, handing the old man a
simple wooden bowl made from the knot in a teak tree.
"Whenever you are hungry, wash the bowl and pray.
Then wish for any food that your heart desires."

"Any food that I want and as *much* as I want?" asked
the old man.

"Any food you want and as much as you want,"
answered the goddess.

The old man wrapped his precious bowl in rags and
began the slow walk home to his wife where they
hugged each other, marvelling at Parvati's generosity.

The old man said to his wife, "Now tell me what you
want to eat."

"How about a sweet mango?"

The old man washed the bowl, prayed and then
wished for a sweet mango. Before he could even finish
his thought, there was the mango sitting in his bowl.

**From 'The Old Man and the Magic Bowl' from *Seasons of Splendour:
Tales, Myths and Legends of India* by Madhur Jaffrey**

31

Thinking back

1 Who are the main characters in this myth?
2 Where do you think the story is set?
3 What kind of character is the old man? What evidence is there of this?
4 What kind of character is the goddess Pavarti?
5 Why is Pavarti so helpful to the old man?
6 What magic events occur because of Pavarti's goodness?

Thinking about it

In this myth, the old man decides to invite the king to dinner to share in his good luck. Continue the story. Use these ideas to help you.

- How do you think the king will react when asked to dinner by the poor old man?
- Will the king be a good or a bad man?
- Will he go to dinner with the old man and his wife?
- He has an evil Prime Minister. How might this Prime Minister take advantage of the old man and his magic bowl?
- How does the old man use Pavarti's bowl at dinner?
- How will Pavarti help the old man against the king and his minister?
- How will things manage to turn out well in the end?

Thinking it through

Write your own myth or legend which explains how one of the following happened.
a) How the zebra got its stripes.
b) Why the sun rises and sets every day.
c) Why crows are black.
- Use copymaster 11 to help you plan your writing. Follow the structure.
- Use description to make the setting clear.
- Use dialogue to make gods, people or animals come to life.

UNIT 12 Writing Myths and Legends – Themes

Think ahead

Every culture in the world has its own myths and legends. Many of these are similar. Which famous myths or legends do you know? Which countries do they come from? What things in them are similar?

Perseus the Gorgon* Slayer

Perseus's grandfather was jealous of him because he was the son of Zeus, king of the gods. This myth tells us about what Perseus did and what happened.

He had a great wooden chest made, and he set Danae in it with the baby in her arms, and pushed it out on to the rippling waters in the Bay of Nauplia.

"It would be a terrible crime to kill my daughter and my grandson," he said, "and the Immortals would send a curse upon me. No, I am merely dispatching them across the sea – and if the waves chance to fill the chest and make it sink, I am not to blame!"

Away floated the chest over the blue sea and out of sight of land; and presently the waves began to rise and the wind to blow, and Danae wept with fear and clasped the baby Perseus close in her arms:

* The Gorgon was a horrible monster with snakes growing out of her hair. If you looked into her eyes, you were turned into stone.

"Oh what a fate is yours," she sobbed, "and yet you do not cry but sleep as peacefully as ever, feeling no terror of the dreadful place in which we are. You do not fear the heaving sea, nor the salt spray on your hair ... Oh, perhaps it is because you know that Father Zeus will protect us ... Then sleep on, sweet babe, for the waves swell only to rock your cradle, and I will pray to Zeus that we may come safely to land."

All night the chest floated over the sea, and in the morning it was washed up on the shores of the island of Seriphos where Polydectes was king. And there Dictys, the king's brother, who was a fisherman, found Danae and her child, and took them to his home and looked after them.

There Perseus grew up, a strong and noble youth skilled in all manner of things from the craft of the fisherman to the use of the sword. In time King Polydectes heard of them, and fell in love with Danae; but she would not marry him, for he was a cruel and wicked tyrant. At length he decided to take her by force; but this he dared not do because Perseus was always there to guard her.

So he devised a scheme to remove Perseus without incurring any blame for killing him. He held a great feast to which he invited the young men of Seriphos, including Perseus, and they all came bringing rich gifts to the King.

But Perseus had nothing to give, and he alone came empty-handed, so that all the young men mocked him, until his cheeks burnt with shame.

"I'll bring a finer present than any of you!" he cried fiercely.

"That cannot be," said cunning Polydectes, "unless you bring me the Gorgon's Head!"

"That I will!" shouted Perseus, "I'll bring it, or die in the attempt!"

And with that he rushed out of the palace amid the loud laughter and jeers of Polydectes and his friends, and went down beside the quiet sea to think what he should do.

While he sat there, deep in thought, two Immortals came to him: Athena, tall and stately in her shining helmet, with her polished shield upon her arm; and Hermes with kindly laughter in his eyes, slim and quick of limb, with the winged sandals on his feet.

"Do not grieve, Perseus," said Hermes, "for, by the will of Zeus, we are come to help you. See, here I lend you the sharpest weapon in the world, that very sickle of adamant with which Cronos wounded the Sky, and which Zeus used in his battle with Typhon. No lesser blade will smite the head from Medusa the Gorgon."

"And I," said Athena in her calm, sweet voice, "will lend you my shield with which I dazzle the eyes of erring mortals who do battle against my wisdom. Any mortal who looks upon the face of Medusa is turned to stone immediately by the terror of it: but if you look only on her reflection in the shield, all will be well."

From *Tales of the Greek Heroes* by Roger Lancelyn Green

Thinking back

1 How did the grandfather hope to kill his grandson?
2 Who found the child and his mother?
3 What kind of person did Perseus grow up to be?
4 How did the wicked King Polydectes trick Perseus?
5 a) Who came to help Perseus?   b) What did they give him to help?

 Thinking about it

1 Make notes from the extract about the main ideas or 'themes' it contains.

> **Themes**
> Someone tries to kill the baby.
> The baby is lost.
> The baby is rescued
> Child grows up in secret.

2 Use copymaster 12 to help you record the main themes of some other myths and legends.

 Thinking it through

1 Write how you think the story continues.
   – How does Perseus meet the Gorgon? What is the Gorgon like?
   – How does he use his magic sword and shield?
   – What happens when he comes back to the wicked king?
2 One of the big themes of myths is that of the Hero. Imagine Perseus is appearing on TV. Write an interview with Perseus in which he is asked about all the heroic things he has done.
   – Will he be big-headed or modest? What will he say to prove this?
   – Why did he do these things? How did he feel about them?
   – What sort of things did he have to do? Who helped him?
   – What were his opponents like? How did he win in the end?
Your interview should be set out like a playscript. You could begin:

> **Interviewer:** (Smiling) Well, Perseus. You are just back from battling with monsters.
> **Perseus:** Yes ... it was no problem really.

UNIT 13 Using the Structure of a Poem

Think ahead

Poems A, B and C are called 'limericks'. What patterns do you notice in them? Poem D is called a 'concrete' poem. Why do you think this is?

A

When Goldilocks left the three bears,
She ran like the wind down the stairs,
"Thank goodness I'm free,"
She shouted with glee,
"But I'm sorry I broke all their chairs!"

B

There was an old man with a beard,
Who said, "It's just as I feared!
Four larks and a wren,
Two owls and a hen,
Have all built their nests in my beard!"

C

There was an old person from Crewe,
Who found a dead mouse in his stew.
Said the waiter, "Don't shout
And wave it about,
Or the rest will be wanting one too!"

D Flying Fish

Flying Fish **by Alan Riddell**

Thinking back

1 How many lines are there in each of poems A, B and C?
2 Which lines rhyme with each other?
3 a) Which lines are long and which are short?
  b) How many syllables do these lines contain?
4 In 'limericks' A, B and C, in which line does the joke come?
5 What shape does the concrete poem D make?

Thinking about it

1 Write a limerick which begins:
  There was a young man from Hong Kong …
  Use the limericks on the previous page as models.
  – Spend time getting the right joke – the 'punch line' – at the end.
2 Write some more limericks. Here are some first lines to help you.
  – *There was a young man from Bengal …*
  – *A furry white rabbit from Tring …*
  Copymaster 13 and the Stepping Stones will help you.

Thinking it through

In poem D, you can tell what the poem is about from its shape. Write a shape poem (concrete poem) called 'The Mosquito'. These ideas will help.
– You are not describing the mosquito in words. You are giving an impression of it using words to create a shape.
– What noise does a mosquito make, for example zzzzzzz? Can you show this sound in one or two letters on the page?
– How does a mosquito move? Can you show this in a shape on the page?
– Plan out all these ideas and then draft the poem.

(Stepping Stones to help you)

• Decide what type of poem you want to write.
• Make rough notes of your ideas and choose only the best ones.
• Check on the ideas, spelling and punctuation and produce a final draft.
(Use copymaster Q to help you.)

UNIT 14 Writing for Different Audiences

Think ahead

Here is a part of a book written for very young children. Can you guess what 'Earthlets' are? What is Dr Xargle really explaining?

Writing for children

The audience for this book is young children. Dr Xargle is from another planet. He explains to other creatures from his planet what 'Earthlets' are and what they do.

1 They have one head and only two eyes, two short tentacles with pheelers on the end and two long tentacles called leggies.

2 They have square claws which they use to frighten off wild beasts known as Tibbles and Marmaduke.

3 Earthlets grow fur on their heads but not enough to keep them warm.

4 They must be wrapped in the hairdo of a sheep.

5 Very old Earthlings (or 'Grannies') unravel the sheep and with two pointed sticks they make Earthlet wrappers in blue and white and pink.

6 Earthlets have no fangs at birth. For many days they drink only milk through a hole in their face.

7 When they have finished the milk they must be patted and squeezed to stop them exploding.

From *Dr Xargle's Book of Earthlets* by Jeanne Willis and Tony Ross

 Thinking back

1 What does Dr Xargle call hands and legs?
2 Why do you think his people do not have words for these things as we do?
3 a) What are the 'wild beasts' in number 2?
   b) How do their names give you a clue?
4 a) What is 'fur' in number 3?
   b) How does the 'hairdo of a sheep' help Earthlets?
5 Can you guess what Dr Xargle is really describing to his people?
6 Do you think this makes a good story for young children?

Thinking about it

Write four more short excerpts from Dr Xargle's Book of Earthlets.
Copymaster 14 will help you plan your pictures and writing.

- Dr Xargle's people have never seen Earthlets before, so even the simplest of things, for example a mouth or legs, needs to be explained.
- Everything the Earthlet does needs to be explained.
- You are writing for an audience of very young children.
- Many of them will not be able to read very well, so use very simple words and short sentences.
- Use pictures to help your audience understand what you are writing about.

Thinking it through

Your audience is now people of your own age.

Imagine you are a Martian and you write a letter home about all the ridiculous things you have seen on Earth in one day. How would you describe these things?

You could include some diagrams with labels. The Stepping Stones will help you.

Because your audience is older you should be letting the words do the work for you, for example, posting a letter could become:

> *I saw the Earthlings pushing some rectangles of a substance they call paper into the mouth of a thin red animal. The beast swallowed it up. Later a man (a doctor?) came and performed an operation. He removed everything from the insides of the creature and ran off down the street.*

Stepping Stones to help you

- Make it clear which age group you are writing for.
- Decide on the type of story.
- Produce a rough draft.
- Use a computer to produce finished text.

(Use copymaster J.)

UNIT 15 Explaining

> **Think ahead**
>
> *It is often difficult to explain something. You have to be clear. You must take your reader through the process step by step. Does the writer need to take you through the process in a certain order?*

Trainer Guide
Choose the right shoes for your sport

You are likely have at least one pair of trainers.

When you buy them do you choose the right ones?

I bet you are thinking: "What? I know what I want!"

OK, but you should check the facts below.

- Running and jumping can damage your joints. Joints like your hips, knees, ankles and toes.
- The right trainers help to protect these joints from damage.
- Finding the best trainers is easy, but you need to know what to look for before you buy.

THE BITS

Trainers are made up of eight parts.

Tongue The tongue should be well padded to prevent rubbing.

Fastening system Laces and straps should be easy to fit and help you make your shoe fit.

Toe wrap The toe wrap should be made from a strong material to protect your toes.

Outer sole The outer soles shouldn't be too stiff, but tough enough to provide grip.

WHAT TO WEAR

A running shoe is lightweight and has a slightly raised heel which reduces stress on your Achilles tendon.

Shoes for off-road running will have a rugged outer and deeper treads. Some will have an outrigger (an extension of the sole which wraps round the ball and heel of your foot). The toe wrap will also be much stronger.

Shoes for basketball or netball, where you are changing direction sharply and jumping, should be light with a high cut which gives your ankle extra support. Midsoles should be well-cushioned and outers should be sturdy.

For aerobics, shoes should be lightweight and have shock absorption in the sole underneath the ball of your foot. The uppers should be mid-cut to give your ankles support. Velcro straps will give your foot stability.

If you play many sports first try a cross trainer. It has a high-cut upper, a firm midsole, and a low, wide base for support.

Inner sole A well-cushioned insole also helps to cope with the force of landing, so should spring back to its first shape each time you take the weight off your foot.

Upper A good sports shoe will have firm uppers which bend, but keep your feet steady and also let your foot move.

Heel counter The heel counter will help to keep the movements of your foot firm and will support the back of your ankle and Achilles tendon, which is easily injured.
So the heel counter should be fairly stiff but allow for easy movement.

Midsole The midsole is one of the most important bits as this is where the cushioning part will be.
Some brands add cushioning parts to increase your spring and 'soak up' the force of your landing.
Some shape their soles to look like the outline of your feet.

From *Manchesterextralink.co.uk*
Internet web site

Thinking back

1 The introductory paragraph does not go into detail about trainers. What does it do?
2 How does the diagram help explain quite difficult things?
3 What is the purpose of explaining these things about trainers to you?
4 How is the explanation divided up? Does this make it easier to read?
5 Find examples of difficult, technical words about training shoes.

Thinking about it

1 Read the passage again. Make notes on:
   a) the different parts that make up a training shoe
   b) the best trainers to wear for different sports.
2 Imagine you have to explain to your sports team why they should be wearing certain kinds of trainers. Write a report for your team captain, stating how trainers are specially made and why it is important to wear the correct ones. You could include diagrams to help you explain. Remember that your audience and purpose is different from the internet article, so your style of writing will need to be different.

Thinking it through

Write an account of a process you know something about, such as loading software onto a computer, or changing a wheel on a bike.
– Use copymaster 15 to help you plan your account.
– Move through the process stage by stage, explaining each part clearly.
– You could use labelled diagrams to make your instructions clearer.
The Stepping Stones will help you.

Stepping Stones to help you

- Introduce the topic in a general way.
- Write the instructions in the correct sequence, from beginning to end.
- Give examples. Link the stages using 'connecting words' to give a sense of time passing, for example, 'then', 'next', 'after that' and so on. (See copymaster K.)
- Write a conclusion.

UNIT 16 Writing from Someone Else's Point of View

Think ahead

The person who tells you a story only gives you his/her point of view. In this story, some city children come to stay with their Aunt in Ireland. What do they think of her? Why?

The first impression of Great-Aunt Dymphna was that she was more like an enormous bird than a great-aunt. This was partly because she wore a black cape, which seemed to flap behind her when she moved. Then her nose stuck out of her thin wrinkled old face just like a very hooked beak. On her head she wore a man's tweed hat beneath which straggled wispy white hair. She wore under the cape a shapeless long black dress. On her feet, in spite of it being a fine warm evening, were rubber boots.

The children gazed at their great-aunt, so startled by her appearance that the polite greetings they would have made vanished from their minds. Naomi was so scared that, though tears went on rolling down her cheeks, she did not make any more noise. Great-Aunt Dymphna had turned her attention to the luggage.

"Clutter, clutter! I could never abide clutter. What have you got in all this?" As she said 'this' a rubber boot kicked at the nearest suitcase.

"Clothes, mostly," said Alex. "Mummy didn't know what we'd need," Penny explained, "so she said we'd have to bring everything."

"Well, as it's here we must take it home, I suppose," said Great-Aunt Dymphna. "Bring it to the car," and she turned and, like a great black eagle, swept out.

Both at London airport and when they had arrived at Cork a porter had helped with the luggage. But now there was no porter in sight and it was clear Great-Aunt Dymphna did not expect that one would be used. Alex took charge.

"You and Naomi carry those two small cases," he said to Robin. "If you could manage one of the big ones, Penny, I can take both mine and then I'll come back for the rest."

Afterwards the children could never remember much about the drive to Reenmore. Great-Aunt Dymphna, in a terrifyingly erratic way, drove the car. It was a large, incredibly old, black Austin. As the children lurched and bounced along – Robin in front, the other three in the back – Great-Aunt Dymphna shot out information about what they met in passing.

"Never trust cows when there's a human with them. Plenty of sense when on their own. Nearly hit that one but only because the stupid man directed the poor beast the wrong way."

As they flashed past farms dogs ran out barking, prepared at risk of their lives to run beside the car.

"Never alter course for a dog," Great-Aunt Dymphna shouted, "just tell him where you are going. It's all he wants." Then, to the dog: "We are going to Reenmore, dear." Her system worked, for at once the dog stopped barking and quietly ran back home.

For other cars or for bicycles she had no respect at all.

"Road hogs," she roared. "Road hogs. Get out of my way or be smashed, that's my rule."

"Oh, Penny," Naomi whispered, clinging to her, "We'll be killed, I know we will."

Penny was sure Naomi was right but she managed to sound brave.

"I expect it's all right. She's been driving all her life and she's still alive."

The only road-users Great-Aunt Dymphna respected were what the children would have called gypsies, but which she called tinkers. They passed a cavalcade of these travelling, not in the gypsy caravans they had seen in England, but in a different type with rounded tops. Behind and in front of the caravans horses ran loose.

"Splendid people, tinkers," Great-Aunt Dymphna shouted. Then, slowing down, she called out something to the tinkers which might, for all the children understood, have been in a foreign language. Then, to the children: "If you need medicine they'll tell you where it grows."

Alex took advantage of the car slowing down to mention the cable.

"We promised Mummy we'd send it," he explained. "And she's sending one to us to say she's arrived and how Daddy is."

"Perhaps a creamery lorry will deliver it sometime," Great-Aunt Dymphna said. "That's the only way a telegram reaches me. You can send yours from Bantry. The post office will be closed, but you can telephone from the hotel."

Penny had no idea what a creamery lorry might be but she desperately wanted her mother's cable.

"Oh, dear, I hope the creamery lorry will be quick, we do so dreadfully want to know how Daddy is."

"Holding his own," Great-Aunt Dymphna shouted. "I asked the seagulls before I came out. They'll tell me if there's any change."

"She's as mad as a coot," Alex whispered to Penny, "I should think she ought to be in an asylum."

Penny shivered.

From *The Growing Summer* by Noel Streatfeild

Thinking back

1 Write down two things that made Aunt Dymphna look like a bird.
2 Why did Naomi cry?
3 What evidence is there in the story to prove that the Aunt's driving was 'erratic'?
4 What do you find strange about the information the Aunt gives the children as they are driving along?
5 a) How did the children want to send a message to their parents?
  b) What was the problem with this?
6 What do the children think of their Aunt?

Thinking about it

1 The children think their Aunt must be mad. Make notes about Aunt Dymphna and find evidence to prove this.
  Copymaster 16 will help you.
2 Write the story of Naomi's adventures with her Aunt in which Aunt Dymphna proves the children are wrong about her.
  – The story could involve the gypsies.
  – It could involve 'medicine' and the gypsies being able to find it.
  – The children have to give up their city ways; they have to enjoy living in the country.
  – Naomi will become brave.

Thinking it through

Write the story from Aunt Dymphna's point of view.
– Say what she thinks of the children.
– Make a list of how the children behave. For example:

> Crying and afraid of things
> Bringing unsuitable clothes
> Not able to carry own luggage
> Not understanding the country

– What does Aunt Dymphna think of the way they behave?
(Note that this is a very old-fashioned story, written when travellers were called 'tinkers' by some people.)

UNIT 17   Imagining Before and After

When you read a story, do you want to know what the characters were like before the story started? In this excerpt, can you imagine what happens next?

The hobbit jumped nearly out of his skin when the hiss came in his ears, and he suddenly saw the pale eyes sticking out at him.

"Who are you?" he said, thrusting his dagger in front of him.

"What iss he, my preciouss?" whispered Gollum (who always spoke to himself through never having anyone else to speak to). This is what he had come to find out, for he was not really very hungry at the moment, only curious; otherwise he would have grabbed first and whispered afterwards.

"I am Bilbo Baggins. I have lost the dwarves and I have lost the wizard, and I don't know where I am; and I don't want to know, if only I can get away."

"What's he got in his handses?" said Gollum, looking at the sword, which he did not like.

"A sword, a blade which came out of Gondolin!"

"Sssss," said Gollum, and became quite polite. "Praps ye sits here and chats with it a bitsy, my preciouss. It like riddles, praps it does, does it?" He was anxious to appear friendly, at any rate for the moment, and until he found out more about the sword and the hobbit, whether he was quite alone really, whether he was good to eat, and whether Gollum was really hungry. Riddles were all he could think of. Asking them, and sometimes guessing them, had been the only game he had ever played with other funny creatures sitting in their holes in the long,

long ago, before he lost all his friends and was driven away, alone, and crept down, down, into the dark under the mountains.

"Very well," said Bilbo, who was anxious to agree, until he found out more about the creature, whether he was quite alone, whether he was fierce or hungry, and whether he was a friend of the goblins.

"You ask first," he said, because he had not had time to think of a riddle.

So Gollum hissed:

> What has roots as nobody sees,
> Is taller than trees
> Up, up it goes,
> And yet never grows?

"Easy!" said Bilbo. "Mountain, I suppose."

"Does it guess easy? It must have a competition with us, my preciouss! If precious asks, and it does not answer, we eats it, my preciouss. If it asks us, and we doesn't answer, then we does what it wants, eh? We show it the way out, yes!"

"All right!" said Bilbo, not daring to disagree, and nearly bursting his brains to think of riddles that could save him from being eaten.

> Thirty white horses on a red hill,
> First they champ,
> Then they stamp,
> Then they stand still.

That was all he could think of to ask – the idea of eating was rather on his mind. It was rather an old one, too, and Gollum knew the answer as well as you do.

"Chestnuts, chestnuts," he hissed. "Teeth! teeth! my preciouss; but we has only six!" Then he asked his second:

Voiceless it cries,
Wingless flutters,
Toothless bites,
Mouthless mutters.

"Half a moment!" cried Bilbo, who was still thinking uncomfortably about eating. Fortunately he had once heard something rather like this before, and getting his wits back he thought of the answer. "Wind, wind of course," he said, and he was so pleased that he made up one on the spot. "This'll puzzle the nasty little underground creature," he thought:

An eye in a blue face
Saw an eye in a green face.
"That eye is like to this eye"
Said the first eye,
"But in low place,
Not in high place."

"Ss, ss, ss," said Gollum. He had been underground a long long time, and was forgetting this sort of thing. But just as Bilbo was beginning to hope that the wretch would not be able to answer, Gollum brought up memories of ages and ages and ages before, when he lived with his grandmother in a hole in a bank by a river, "Sss, sss, my preciouss," he said. "Sun on the daisies it means, it does."

But these ordinary above ground everyday sort of riddles were tiring for him. Also they reminded him of days when he had been less lonely and sneaky and nasty, and that put him out of temper. What is more they made him hungry; so this time he tried something a bit more difficult and more unpleasant...

From *The Hobbit* by JRR Tolkien

Thinking back

1 a) Who are the characters in this extract?   b) Where are they?
2 What are the characters like?
3 What is Gollum afraid of when he meets the Hobbit?
4 What does Bilbo Baggins say that shows he has not always been alone?
5 Gollum remembers where he used to live a long time ago.
  Where was that?
6 How does the last line of the passage tell you that the story will be
  turning nastier?

Thinking about it

1 Tell the story of Gollum and how you think he came to be the nasty
  creature he seems in this passage.
  – Look for clues in the passage that will tell you about his past.
  – Who were the creatures he used to riddle with?
  – Why did he have to leave his hole in a bank by a river?
    Was it because of something he did?
  – Who or what drove him away into the dark of the mountains?
  – What happened to his grandmother?
  – Do you feel sorry for him because he is lonely?
  – Is he really 'sneaky' and 'nasty'?
  Copymaster 17 will help you plan your ideas.
2 Now tell the story of the Hobbit in the same way.

Thinking it through

The Hobbit and Gollum have a competition, telling riddles for their lives.
Continue the story.
– What do you think happens next?
– What riddles do they tell each other?
– Who wins?
– What happens to Gollum?
– What happens to the Hobbit?

UNIT 18 Performance Poems

Hundreds of years ago, before so many people could read, poetry was spoken or chanted. This is a modern poem which is meant to be 'performed' – acted out. How would people remember the words of a poem such as this? What kinds of actions would go with it? How would the rhythm of the poem help in the performance?

Come Zipporah come rock with I
Songs of praise to set spirit high,
Drummers beat, drummers beat,
We were never here to stay
Hear that sound from far away,
Drummers beat, drummers beat,
Beat drummers beat 'cause the beat well sweet
Beat down the beat that cools the heat,
Drummers beat, drummers beat.

Come little children rock with I
The beat of the drum will never die,
Drummers beat, drummers beat,
Drum beat sound will never drown
Listen to the beat as the beat beats a hard,
Drummers beat, drummers beat,
Beat drummers beat and beat it hard
Beat it like you beat it when you beat it back a yard,
Drummers beat, drummers beat,
Beat drummers, beat drummers beat drummers beat.

From *Beat Drummers* by Benjamin Zephaniah

Thinking back

1 Which line is repeated as a 'chorus' every two lines?
2 Find two examples of slang words in the poem which show the poem is meant to be spoken rather than read.
3 This poem is often spoken by a narrator. Everyone joins in with certain lines. Which lines do you think would be best for this?
4 Which words would sound good if they were shouted out?

 Thinking about it

1 Use the pattern of the poem:

The first two lines rhyme ⟶ { *Come Zipporah come rock with I*
Common expressions are used   { *Songs of praise to set spirit high,*
The third line is a repetition ⟶ *Drummers beat, drummers beat,*
of a phrase

Write six more lines of the poem about another musical instrument.
  – Think about what it sounds like. For example, *a trumpet blares, a saxophone wails, a violin screams*
  – Think about the rhythm of the instrument. This poem imitates drums. What rhythm would a triangle use?
2 Perform the verses. Use the Stepping Stones to help you.
  – You could have a performance poem about an entire orchestra!

 Thinking it through

Write another performance poem. Copymaster 18 will give you some ideas. Explain why it is a good poem to perform.
  – The poem you write should be lively.
  – It should have a good rhythm or use great words.
  – You should be able to make it come to life with your voices.

Stepping Stones to help you

• Decide which parts of the poem will be fast and which parts will be slow.
• Decide how you will divide up the poem between you.
• Talk about what kind of feeling you want to get into each part.
• Select the words in the poem you want to stress.
(Use copymaster L to help you.)

UNIT 19 Letters for Real Purposes

Think ahead

We often need to write letters to explain that we feel strongly about something or to persuade people. What is the purpose of this letter? How do you tell if someone is giving you facts, or just his/her point of view?

43 Green Road
Henfold
ENX 123

2nd February

Dear Sir,

I believe that recycling rubbish is very important.
    Collecting and disposing of rubbish costs money. If it wasn't collected, then it would be left to pollute the environment. Before long we would be buried in our own waste.
    It is cheaper to use reclaimed materials. Not only are they cheaper, but they save the world's resources.
    Many charities get money from recycling. They sell bottles, cans, tin foil and paper to industry for recycling.
    But Britain is still not as far ahead as other countries when it comes to recycling waste and saving resources. We need to do something about this and make people aware of the facts.

    Yours faithfully,

    Mrs M Steven

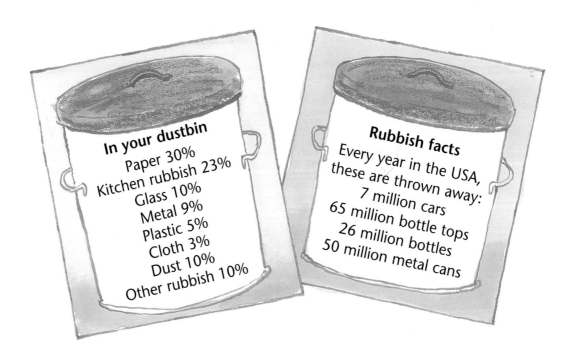

In your dustbin
Paper 30%
Kitchen rubbish 23%
Glass 10%
Metal 9%
Plastic 5%
Cloth 3%
Dust 10%
Other rubbish 10%

Rubbish facts
Every year in the USA, these are thrown away:
7 million cars
65 million bottle tops
26 million bottles
50 million metal cans

Recycling information

Materials	Amount recycled	Savings
Glass	150 000 tonnes per year. 10% of our waste.	Saves on fuel. Less fuel is needed to make glass from recycling.
Paper products	2 million tonnes per year.	1 tonne saves 14 trees.
Tin cans	9% of our waste. One third recycled.	Saves energy. Less energy needed to make cans from recycling than from metal ore.

 Thinking back

1 How do you know that the passage on page 55 is a letter?
2 How can you tell that it is written to someone Mrs Steven does not know well?
3 What two things does the author say will happen if we do not collect and dispose of rubbish?
4 Which groups of people benefit from recycling?

Thinking about it

Imagine you are writing a letter to your local newspaper. Give facts about:
a) the amount of rubbish we create in the world;
b) how much we save by recycling.
– Use the information from the charts and diagrams to help you.
– Will your letter look better if it is word-processed?

> Nelson House
> Mayfield Road
> Walton-on-Thames
> 1st April
>
> Dear Sir,
> I agree with Mrs Steven about recycling waste. Your readers might like to know the following facts ...

 Thinking it through

Imagine you are writing to your local MP. Write a letter saying that recycling is a waste of time and money. You will need to think of opposite arguments to Mrs Steven.
– Draw a chart like this to help you plan your argument.

Arguments in favour of recycling waste	Arguments against recycling waste

– Draft your letter carefully before producing a final version.
  Use copymaster 19 and the Stepping Stones to help you.

Stepping Stones to help you

- Decide whether you want to write an official letter or an informal letter.
- The style should match the type of letter.
- How will you begin? How will you end it?
- Always put your address and the date.
- Check the presentation, spelling and punctuation.
(Use copymaster P to help you.)

UNIT 20   Writing a News Report

Think ahead

We look to newspapers to give us information, but we have to be careful. Writers can just give us their version of what happened. How much of this report do you think is fact? How much is just the opinion of the writer?

DOUBLE GOAL SURPRISE IN CLOSING MINUTES

Caistor Town 3
Walthamstow Rovers 0

Red and white scarves were flying over the town yesterday to celebrate the team's long-deserved victory.

Spectators at Saturday's exciting match in Caistor must have been well-satisfied. They saw a game in which the home team always had the better of the play. But the result was not decided until ex-schoolboy player Tommy Smith neatly scored two brilliant goals in the final minutes. Although tempers did become worse towards the end, referee Barker controlled the game well.

Blond-haired, popular Fitzpatrick opened the scoring in the eighth minute when he chased a pass from his new team-mate Sharpe and easily shot past the goalkeeper. The part-time players from Walthamstow just stood appealing for offside instead of tackling. Their angry protests were firmly and wisely dealt with by the referee.

The game remained even until half time. After that, the home team were by far the better side. In the fiftieth minute, eighteen-year-old Parkinson had to head the ball off the goal, although this was one of the rare times the Rovers looked like scoring.

Gentle giant felled by blow

Then, in the seventieth minute, the six-foot tall Tomkins of Walthamstow was sent off. Mick Moorcroft, known to his friends as 'the gentle giant', tackled. Tomkins fell, but as Moorcroft turned to help, Tomkins struck him in the face. The referee had no choice but to show him the red card and send him off.

Being one man short was too much for Walthamstow. Caistor mounted attack after attack. Despite some wild kicking by Walthamstow's defence, Caistor could not score. Then, with some fog coming down, Smith scored his two clever goals in the last five minutes. The first came after he had been felled by a desperate tackle. Smith easily converted the penalty. The second came from a fifteen yard kick which moved so fast that the stunned goalie could not even move to save it.

Manager Bob Lawson told us that he knew the team could do it. He said that they just needed a chance.

"I'll be back next week," said Mick Moorcroft, bravely, "When this cut heals up. You can't keep a good team down!"

Thinking back

1 a) Which teams were playing?   b) Where was the match played?
2 Do you think this writer supported Caistor or Walthamstow? Why?
3 Look at the sub-heading in the report. What impression does it give you about Tomkins and whose fault the incident was?
4 What evidence can you find that shows this was a bad-tempered match?

Thinking about it

Write a short news report about the incident in the match when Tomkins was sent off.
– Make notes about what happened. Invent some more details.

> Where did the match take place? What was the weather like?
> When did the incident happen? Which people were involved?
> Whose fault was it? What actually happened?
> What was the result?
> What are your feelings as a reporter about the incident?

Thinking it through

Write a news report about the same match, but imagine you support Walthamstow. What differences would there be?
– You need to show how you like Walthamstow and not Caistor.
– Decide which details will change and which details will remain the same.
– What is your view of the incidents?
– Copymaster 20 will help you organise your ideas.
– Use the Stepping Stones to help with the style of a news report.

Stepping Stones to help you

• Think about the sort of language you need to use for the article, for example does a football report use special 'football language'?
• Write a headline which will attract attention.
• Your first paragraph should introduce the article.
• Include direct and indirect speech as if you have interviewed people.
(Use copymaster M to help you.)

UNIT 21 Writing a Leaflet

Think ahead

Leaflets are meant to tell us important things in a simple and attractive way. How important is it that they should be brief? Should they have pictures to make the idea clearer? How can they best give you difficult information in a simple way?

Come to the ONE AND ONLY

VICTORIAN TOYS MUSEUM

Westbury Mead Village

Go back to Victorian times

*

See all the toys in their historical settings

*

'AWARD-WINNING'

*

'UNIQUE'

*

'UNMISSABLE!'

AS SHOWN ON T.V.

It's world famous - and deserves to be!
ABC News

Come and visit the award-winning Victorian Toys Museum, described by one reviewer as 'the most fascinating museum I have ever been to'. Situated in a Victorian house, over four floors, in historical settings.

* Marvel at the old dolls – some of them the size of real babies and children!
* Play with the clockwork machines.
* Move the soldiers around on their fields of battle.
* Play the musical instruments.
* See the teddy bear weddings.
* Look at the huge, detailed dolls' houses.

You'll have the time of your life!

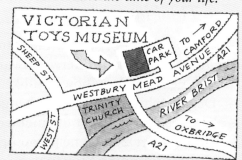

Victorian Toys Museum
44 Westbury Mead Avenue,
Westbury Mead, Bristbury.
Tel: 1234 88999544
Email: victorian.toys@westbury.co.uk
FOR FREE MAIL ORDER CATALOGUE
CALL US OR WRITE!

OPEN EVERY DAY OF THE YEAR

VISIT OUR SPECIAL SHOP TOO!
AND OUR CAFÉ! WE SERVE SPECIAL
VICTORIAN SWEETS AND PUDDINGS

Air conditioned
Founder member: Anna Jones

Thinking back

1 Why is it important to have a picture on the front of a leaflet?
2 What do the words 'one and only' tell you?
3 What other words on the leaflet tell you what others have said about the museum? Why is important to print some of them on the front?
4 Why is it important to have a map on the leaflet?

Thinking about it

Write a leaflet for new parents about your school. Follow the pattern of the Victorian Toys leaflet. Use the list below to help you.

Headline	Picture
People's views about the school	A brief description
How to find the school	Essential information
Important people at the school	

– You may need to do some research.
– You could design the leaflet. What shape will it be? What pictures or drawings will it need? Copymaster 21 will help you plan your leaflet.

Thinking it through

Write a leaflet to persuade people to contribute money towards an animal rescue centre.
– What sort of rescue centre will you write about?
– What will you say about the work it does and the need for it?
– How will pictures help?
Remember to use persuasive language. Copymaster 21 will help you.

Stepping Stones to help you

• Decide upon a main heading or headline for the leaflet.
• Decide upon a subheading or clever catch phrase.
• Be clear about the main message of the leaflet. What are you aiming to do?
• Make the message easy to understand. Use bullet points and pictures.
• Use details to make your point more interesting.
• Write a brief final statement.
(Use copymaster N to help you.)

UNIT 22 Presenting your Case

Think ahead

When you feel strongly about something, you may want to write about it to give your point of view. What is the best way to make somebody understand how you feel? How does this poster help to present the case in this unit?

A **Do you think that fireworks celebrations every November 5th should be banned?**

B   **Anna wrote the good and bad points of firework celebrations.**

Fireworks celebrations
Good points
* They are fun.
* They are beautiful.
* Fireworks parties bring people together.
* Bonfires get rid of rubbish.
* They raise money for charity.
* There are very few injuries every year.
* Training is provided for police and ambulances.
* Fireworks give pleasure.
* November 5th is a tradition.
* They teach children to be careful and responsible.

Fireworks celebrations
Bad points
* They cause injuries.
* They cause fires.
* They keep people awake.
* They are noisy.
* They are a waste of money.
* They pollute our environment.
* They are dangerous.
* They scare dogs and cats.
* Most people don't know why they are celebrating.
* They encourage children to beg.

Thinking back

1 Why do you think the poster on page 62 uses such a lot of:
  a) capital letters?   b) exclamation marks?
2 How can you tell which is the most important message of the poster?
3 The rocket is made to look like a person telling you the rules. Who do you think this poster is aimed at?
4 How does Anna, the writer of B, make her points easy to read?

 Thinking about it

Use the information on the notepads on page 63. Write out the arguments for and against celebrating bonfire night.
– Copymaster 22 will help you to organise your ideas.
– Combine the ideas and write in paragraphs.
– Use words to link the ideas, for example 'of course', 'however', 'some people believe that', 'but', 'it is my belief that', and so on.

 Thinking it through

Use the information on the poster.
Design a poster like the one on page 62 for the Anti Fireworks Society (AFS). Make the case that fireworks can be deadly and should be banned. The poster is to be given to children in schools. Make some notes first.

Instruction	Danger
Keep fireworks in a closed box.	A spark might get in the box and set them all off.

– Think about making the language simple.
– How will you use pictures to help?

Stepping Stones to help you

• Write an opening statement. This is what you believe.
• Write your arguments. Take one at a time. Give examples for each one.
• Say what other people believe.
• Give a summary of your view at the end.
(Use copymaster R to help you.)